BR DIESELS DOUBLEHEADED

BR DIESELS DOUBLEHEADED

G. WEEKES

D. BRADFORD BARTON LIMITED

Frontispiece: the two LMSR 1600 bhp diesel-electrics, designed by H. G. Ivatt in conjunction with English Electric, were designed from the outset for use in pairs and after Nationalisation they became familiar sights on such famous expresses as 'The Royal Scot.' No. 10000 – Willesden shed's first main line diesel – heads sister 10001 up the climb of Shap with the down service on a June day in 1957. [R. H. Leslie]

 771/3NB *ISBN 0 85153 301 9*
printed in Great Britain by H. E. Warne Ltd, London and St. Austell
for the publishers

D. BRADFORD BARTON LTD · Trethellan House · Truro · Cornwall · England

introduction

Doubleheading, that is the use of two locomotives at the head end of a train, was in steam days a sign of some degree of inefficiency in railway operation from one cause or another. It might be a lack of sufficiently powerful locomotives to work the traffic, perhaps a breakdown, or simply heavy gradients. Yet this is not the case in the present era of the diesel when the availability and utilisation of motive power follows a rather different pattern.

First and foremost, use of two diesels does not involve the provision of two crews; nor does an excess number of locomotives to cope with traffic peaks involve the costly provision of sheds for them as would be the case with the far less easily serviced steam locomotive. Moreover, diesels are essentially mixed traffic machines and it makes good sense to use the smaller Type 1s or 2s singlehanded on short-distance local passenger specials. Admittedly not all BR main line diesel classes can be coupled together as regards their controls, in order to be run in multiple (i.e. both locomotives under the control of one driver) but this is one of the aims of the standardisation of the classes that has been proceeding for some time. Locomotives with dissimilar controls have to be used in tandem, i.e. with a driver in each, but this practice is rapidly becoming rarer. Multiple coupling of two locomotives takes perhaps fifteen minutes to make the necessary jumper connections and tests; thereafter two 1250 hp units (or one of 1000 and one of 1500 hp) are transformed into one 2500 hp unit of equal efficiency – an obvious point until one considers this in comparison to the far less efficient pairing of two steam locomotives where by no means an X2 factor was achieved as regards drawbar-horsepower.

Abroad, particularly in the United States, the concept of using diesel units in multiple is the norm, merely adding horsepower upon horsepower to reach whatever is needed for the load or the grade. In this way three, four, five or even six head-end diesels may work a train – quite apart from slave-controlled mid-train helpers plus a unit or two at the rear – to utilise the availability of a pool of motive power to the full. On BR, where very different conditions apply, anything beyond the use of two head-enders is rare on any Region; the Perth-Inverness main line sees occasional trios of Class 24/25/26s on the heavier passenger trains, whilst Lickey incline provides an English example of the multi-diesel lash-up which is commonplace in North America. Elsewhere in Britain even triple-headers are rare to say the least and invariably the result of a failure of one of the locomotives concerned. Occasionally a string of diesels may be seen running light engine outside depot limits but in these cases it is almost always the situation that the leading unit only is powered and the others are dead, i.e. being towed.

The general layout of this volume will soon be apparent for it commences with the efficient, ubiquitous and hardworking Class 20 Type 1s and progresses through the Types 2 and 3 upwards through the power range. Inevitably Type 2s predominate, for this reflects the fact that the majority of doubleheading by diesels in recent years on BR is the result of making two 1250 hp Type 2s into a 2500 hp Type 4. The continuing change in freight traffic patterns on BR, with longer-distance heavier block workings replacing the former 'mixed goods', has rendered Type 2s over-abundant and Type 4s – particularly since the oil crisis of 1973 – in short supply. Relatively few doubleheading combinations due to straightforward failures have been included in the volume, partly because of the plethora of these and partly because they are not truly representative of diesels doubleheaded in day-to-day working.

10000

Repainted in their later colour scheme of dark green with pale stripe along the body, the Ivatt pair did not look quite as soberly impressive as they had in the earlier all black livery but they nevertheless impressed the top link West Coast footplatemen who did a shift in the comfort of their cab, compared to the 'office' on a draughty rattling 8P Pacific – or even worse a bucking 7P 'Royal Scot', which if it got a chance would throw you to the floor . . . The '10000 pair' have power almost off as they sweep effortlessly south near Shap Wells on 6 July 1958. [R. H. Leslie]

Interchange took place in the mid-1950s between Southern and LM Region of their main line diesels, to give greater experience to British Railways, ready for the impending wholesale change to the new form of motive power; the two earlier Southern units, numbered 10201 and 10202, are here seen on the up 'Royal Scot' north of Carlisle in December 1957. Built at Ashford Works to designs by Bulleid and using EE main components, they were greatly overweight by modern standards – 135 tons apiece for only 1600 bhp, but nevertheless they contributed usefully to BR main line diesel development.

[R. H. Leslie]

When the first of the new Type 1 diesel-electrics appeared on London Midland Region in 1957 they were put on duties which were quite different from those they later saw. Dark green-liveried Nos. 8000 and 8003 are here coming south through Rugby with a fast freight on the West Coast main line, 23 July 1959. They are new enough to arouse interest in the crew of superannuated 0-6-0 No. 58218 shunting on the right. [M. J. Jackson]

▷ The numerous English Electric Class 20 diesels make a very handy 2000 hp combination when worked in pairs and are frequently seen in this way in the east Midlands; Class 20s Nos. 20 043 and 20 070 leaving Cliff Hill sidings to cross High Street level crossing at Coalville in Leicestershire with loaded coal wagons, 17 July 1974. Certain of the class have not had reporting headcode boxes fitted and still use the original hinged-flap marker discs. [P. D. Hawkins]

LEISURE

Nos. 8172 and 8188 rumble past Horninglow Bridge at Burton-on-Trent with a block train of oil fuel tanks, 31 May 1972. The majority of the class are allocated to LM Region's Nottingham Division with others on Scottish and Eastern Regions. Under ER's initial diesel classification they were coded 10/3. [P. J. Rose]

Nos. 20 047 and 20 046, with a freight for Gloucester, start the descent of Lickey bank at Blackwell on 24 August 1975. The working of 'inclines' has changed somewhat since the days of steam. [D. E. Canning]

D8184 and D8143 at Westhouses Yard on 20 January 1969 with coal empties. The trailing locomotive has the intermediate type of small yellow warning panel seen before all-yellow ends became standard. [Norman E. Preedy]

The great majority of paired Class 20s run with cabs outermost, as the forward visibility of these Type 1s is otherwise as bad as it used to be with steam locomotives. And once crews have become used to a well nigh unrestricted view of the track ahead they dislike a Class 20 other than cab-first. Nos. 20 126 and 20 104 are two of the many used for local freights in the industrial parts of Scotland and are seen on an eastbound transfer freight on 30 September 1974.
[D. G. Cameron]

irs of 20s are pressed into use in summer to work weekend specials, although they have slight disadvantages of a 75 ph maximum speed and a smaller than standard (400 gallon) fuel capacity; Nos.8305 and 8307, on a change from coal ins, leaving Bridlington with a Scarborough-Sheffield passenger train, 4 September 1971. [P. J. Rose]

Nos. 20 044 and 20 135 have full power on for the Camp Hill line climb with a southbound freight, at St. Andrews Junction, Birmingham on 10 April 1975. The train has just come under the main line to Euston which the Class 25 – with a parcels train for Curzon Street – is about to join.
[P. D. Hawkins]

Renumbering of the Class 20s has been a simple matter, of substituting the prefix 20 for the first figure of 8 except in the case of the later 8300-27 series which lost 100 in their renumbering, becoming the equivalent of 8200-27 (the BTH 800 hp Type 1s which originally bore that batch of numbers being now extinct). Here Nos. 20 162 (formerly 8162) and 20 197 (formerly 8197) pass Chesterfield 'light engine', on 22 September 1974. [Norman E. Preedy]

8V62
20147

Two Class 20s pack not only a 2000 hp 'punch' but also 70 tons of brake force and are thus even better suited to working heavy loose-coupled freights than say the 'Peaks'. This is particularly the case as they can take 3½ chain minimum curves compared to 5 chains for the latter and this makes them suitable also for working in and out of colliery sidings. Nos. 20 147 and 20 067 approach Horton Road crossing at Gloucester with a loaded coal train on 16 August 1974. [Norman E. Preedy]

The first few North British diesel-hydraulics of the D63xx series, introduced in 1959, were actually only 1000 hp machines and thus, like the D80xx series, were really Type 1s according to BR original power range designation (Type 1 800-1000 hp: Type 2 1000-1365 hp: Type 3 1500-1750 hp: Type 4 2000-2500 hp) but from D6306 onwards a slightly uprated version of the NBL/MAN engine gave a power output of 1100 hp. Assuredly this was seldom as reliable or as strong an output as the trusty 8SVT engine in the EE product. D6314 and D6315 are here on a running-in trip returning to Swindon from Gloucester on their first day in traffic, on 25 January 1960. The setting is Kemble, with a railbus visible at the platform serving the Cirencester branch. [M. J. Jackson]

Two D63xx class, with D6304 leading, bring an up express into St. Erth in Cornwall on a July day in 1959. The first six in the series (with 1100 hp engines) could not be worked in multiple with the later ones and the two seen here are working in tandem.

[P. Q. Treloar]

The Derby-designed and built Type 2s with Sulzer engines and BTH electrics were a success from the outset. Later known as Class 24, they were numbered in the D50xx series. Nos. 5031 and 5035, from the Stoke (D5) Division and working out of Birkenhead, head one of the iron-ore trains from Bridston Dock there towards Shotton steelworks near Chester, and are seen passing Seacombe Junction signal box. Prominent on the side of the eleven big bogie hopper wagons is the name of the owning steel company. 9F 2-10-0s were the predecessors of the Class 24s on this traffic. [David H. Allan]

Nos. 24 006 and 24 105 approaching Perth on 3 May 1975 with a train of cement hoppers for Inverness. In the distance can be seen Moncreiffe Tunnel, beyond which is the junction where the Glasgow and Edinburgh routes diverge. Perth has always been an important route centre, with the Dundee, Aberdeen and Inverness lines converging here from the north; the layout of the station and its environs was carried out in the early 1960s, including power signalling and the provision of a new marshalling yard.
[D. G. Cameron]

An excursion from Leamington Spa leaving Paignton in March 1975 behind Nos. 25 038 and 25 188: below, the empty stock of the Royal Train behind Nos. 25 051 and 25 053 at Wadborough on the Birmingham - Gloucester line on 28 May 1975, *en route* from Wolverton to Bristol. [G. F. Bannister]

Class 25 No. 7677 and Class 52 No. 1026 *Western Centurion* ease through the speed restriction into Saltash station in Cornwall with a string of empty ballast hoppers eastbound for Stoneycombe quarries, 31 May 1973. These two classes cannot be run in multiple and both locomotives are manned. [G. F. Gillham]

A pair of Class 25s is probably the most common doubleheaded diesel combination to be seen anywhere in Britain; Class 25/2 No. 25 245 and Class 25/1 No. 25 082 head through Aspatria on the Workington - Carlisle line in August 1975.
[M. J. Jackson]

One of the Laira-based Class 25s, D7577 helps ailing 'Warship' No. 812 *Royal Naval Reserve 1859-1959* through Saltash with the up 'Cornishman', having been attached at Bodmin Road. [David H. Allan]

Soon after being transferred to Western Region (to Cardiff Canton) from the Midlands, No. 7504 pilots Class 52 No. 1002 *Western Explorer* through Newton Abbot on an up milk train from Cornwall, 19 July 1972. [G. F. Gillham]

Type 2s are valuable mixed-traffic machines which are ideal for any duties from local trip freights single-handed to long distance excursions when worked in pairs. Freight duties on weekdays and passenger duties at weekends are the summer norm for many LM Region 25s, as with Nos. 5270 and 5223 at Skegness with an excursion from Leicester on 6 August 1972. [Norman E. Preedy]

Two of Laira's Class 25s, Nos. 7625 and 7676, head over the viaduct towards North Road station at Plymouth on 1 September 1973 with the 12.45 Penzance to Cardiff. They will probably come off here and be replaced by a Type 4, either a 'Western' or a Class 47. The increased maximum speed of these later small BR-Sulzers, of 90 mph, compared to 75 in the case of the lower-geared earlier ones (Class 24) makes them more valuable for extended main line use.

[P. D. Hawkins]

The 15.05 from St. Pancras to Sheffield bursts out of Elstree Tunnel behind Class 25s Nos. 7562 and 5293. Opposite, another Sheffield - St. Pancras train, at the same locality, behind No. 7616 in two-tone green livery and No. 5281 in blue. Both photographs date from June 1973. [Brian Morrison]

1C51

30 All over Britain, the Class 24/25 workhorses emit their sturdy Sulzer throb; Class 24/25 Nos. 5120 and 5124 pass Ferryhill, south of Aberdeen, with 'The Night Capitals', the 23.15 sleeper from Kings Cross. These two Inverness locomotives are on this turn probably due to the customary 47 having failed *en route.* [Brian Morrison]

A Sunday morning scene at Sleaford in Lincolnshire, with doubleheaders Class 25/3 No. 7614 (now 25 264) and No. 7619 (now 25 269) holding up the traffic at the level crossing prior to their departure with the 08.50 Leicester - Skegness, run on Sundays only during the summer service. [C. J. Ferris]

6M31
25272

Two of the then new Western Region allocation of ex-Midland Class 25s, D7518 and D7159, haul an up freight through Newport on the centre road on 5 October 1972. [G. F. Gillham]

A pair of visiting Class 25s, including No. 25 272, wait at the bufferstops at Aberystwyth having brought in an excursion from the Midlands in August 1975. Below, two Class 24s make a vigorous start away from the terminus with the 10.10 through train to Euston, August 1972. The Vale of Rheidol tracks are in the left foreground. [J. Reeves]

Highland Class 24s at Inverness; Nos. 5124 and 5113 with a train of North Sea gas pipes for Aberdeen on 1 April 1974. [Brian Morrison]

Nos. 24 143 and 24 037 take the Crewe line at Kidsgrove with a coal train from Stoke-on-Trent, 17 April 1975. [P. D. Hawkins]

There is probably more doubleheading in the regular course of events on the Glasgow-Inverness route than anywhere else on BR, with a combination of Class 24/25/26/27 units working in pairs. Here, Nos. 26 040 and 26 018 are leaving Queen Street (Glasgow) on 19 July 1975 with the 09.35 to Inverness. [D. G. Cameron]

A combination of diesels one is seldom likely to see occurred in April 1969 when D9019 *Royal Highland Fusilier* was specially booked to run a military special train south from Inverness to Aldershot. It worked north from Perth, with Class 26 No. 5338 on the 'Highland Mail' consisting of only seven vehicles, resulting in a fast run, needless to say. The pair are here waiting time at Aviemore. Two other photographs of this unusual doubleheader, also taken by Derek Cross, occur in his admirable volume in the series, *BR Diesels in the Landscape.* [Derek Cross]

The 08.20 Inverness - Edinburgh departs from Perth on 3 May 1975 headed by the customary pair of Type 2s, on this occasion Class 24/1 No. 24 118, and Class 26/1 No. 26 035 – both Inverness locomotives. Truly has it been said that the Sulzer 6LDA-28 engine conquered the Highlands, for they have a virtual monopoly everywhere north of Perth and Glasgow. [D. G. Cameron]

An unidentified pair of BR-Sulzer Type 2s near the summit of Druimachdar with the 11.25 Inverness - Perth on 18 October 1972. A six-coach load is well within a single Class 25's capability over the route but many of the Inverness allocation are left semi-permanently coupled in pairs: 12 bogies are regarded as the maximum load for a pair of Type 2s and above these three locomotives are used.

[D. E. Canning]

Paired Type 2s are seen on the Aberdeen services as well as the more customary Type 4s, as with Nos. 26 019 and 26 010 seen here crossing the River Esk viaduct out of Montrose with the 13.15 from Aberdeen to Glasgow via Dundee, 30 March 1974.

[Brian Morrison]

Another BRCW doubleheader, seen at Newtonmore on 21 June 1967; D5328 and D5333 with an afternoon up train wait for another incoming Class 26 with a Perth - Inverness train. These 53xx were originally an allocation to Eastern and LM Region but were concentrated at Inverness and Eastfield after trials had shown their suitability for Highland conditions. [Norman E. Preedy]

Edinburgh (Waverley), 11 September 1974; the driver of Nos. 24 070 and 26 023 opens up the 2,300-odd combined horsepower with the 13.40 to Inverness. Contrary to popular opinion, it is not weight restriction that accounts for the use of multiple Type 2s on the Highland main line; Class 40s, 45/46s, 47s, 50s and even Class 55s can work as far north as Inverness without special restriction.
[D. G. Cameron]

One of Haymarket's 26s, No. 26 014, heading back north for Carlisle as helper to EE Class 40 No. 40 009, 2 September 1975. Their train, 8P44, is a freight from Workington.
[M. J. Jackson]

Two of the older Class 24s, Nos. 5099 and 5090, slam through Newtonmore in the wide vale of Strathspey on 18 August 1973 with a lengthy Invergordon - Glasgow cruise special. Early Class 24s are now in process of being withdrawn, and scrapped at Swindon works.
[Derek Cross]

Eastern Region's stalwart and standard Type 2 is the Brush-built Class 31 first introduced in 1957. A rather ponderous and heavy A1A-A1A with a noticeably low power-weight ratio, it gave some trouble in the intermediate Mirrlees-engined versions (uprated to 1365 or 1600 hp) but nevertheless it was responsible for much of the pioneer success of ER dieselisation. This scene at Rotherham (Masboro') is of D5848 and D5832 passing though with a train of coal empties, with 9F ex-Crosti 2-10-0 No. 92029 also visible on the left.
[A. J. Booth]

A pair of Class 31s in original green livery passing Angle Lane with a Ripple Lane-Whitemoor fitted freight on 9 November 1963. Perhaps the best looking version of the minor variations of this design was the original series without headcode panel on the roofends; in white striped green livery with grey roof, black underframe and white route discs, they were striking! [P. Paye]

8F51
5845

7V89
D5836

The difference in appearance between earlier and later liveried Class 31s is shown by Nos. 5845 and 5826 on a coal train at Toton, 10 June 1969. BR lost its enthusiasm for anything except a plain overall livery in the late 1960s, presumably convinced that such niceties as striped livery – and nameplates – were not in keeping with the ultra-modern utilitarian attitude they should have for traction units. [Norman E. Preedy]

The 50 mph speed restriction imposed through Burton-on-Trent, due to the curves on the lines through the station, matters little to Class 31 Nos. 5660 and 5681 as they pass slowly through in the down direction with a loaded train of house coal, 31 May 1972. [Peter J. Rose]

Another pair of blue-and-green liveried Class 31s; Nos. 5836 and 5823 passing Chesterfield on 9 November 1968 with a Scunthorpe-Severn Tunnel Junction train conveying steel strip. Brake force of a Class 31 is high, reflecting its all-up weight of 109 tons – much the same as a Class 52 'Western' and this made them ideal for loose-coupled heavy freights such as this. [Peter J. Rose]

Class 31 Nos. 31 295 and 31 291 ease the 12.34 Worcester to Paddington (via Birmingham) over the Birmingham - Derby main line, approaching St Andrews Junction and the Camp Hill line to gain the ex-GWR metals at Small Heath; 30 May 1974. [P. D. Hawkins]

Western Region now has Class 31s to replace the much-lamented 'Hymeks'; Nos. 31 259 and 31 258 passing Lapworth with the 06.45 Paddington - Birmingham (New Street) on 21 June 1975. [P. D. Hawkins]

Class 31s regularly haul the Royal Train; on Eastern Region Nos. 5659 and 5639, from Stratford, exhibit the Royal Train 1X01 headcode as they head east from Liverpool Street towards Kings Lynn on a snowy 28 December 1968, conveying HM the Queen and family *en route* to Sandringham. [P. Paye]

Southern Region's own diesel class is the Type 3 BRCW-Sulzer of 1550 hp, now Class 33, which is a slightly enlarged version of the Type 2 used in Scotland. Two of the class, Nos. 6530 and 6527, doublehead a Waterloo - Exeter express westward out of Salisbury in December 1973.
[G. F. Gillham]

Doubleheading on the Southern is relatively rare compared to say LM Region but one normal turn on which two Class 33s might be see is the 08.50 Brighton to Exeter on Saturdays. Two of the narrow-bodied Class 33/2 diesels, D6594 and D6586, are seen here headin through Wilton on 7 September 1968. It is unusual to see these Hastings line locomotives so far west. Below; the same train, loaded t something like 14 bogies, at Gillingham in Dorset on an August Saturday in 1970 behind D6566 and D6558.
[G. F. Gillham/G. F. Banniste

G2

G2

D6517 pilots Class 47 D1683 between Alton and Medstead on a Waterloo - Weymouth express on a Sunday in June 1966. All Waterloo - Bournemouth - Weymouth trains were diverted from Winchester Junction via Alton - Farnham - Aldershot to Woking (and reverse direction) at this time owing to work on the main line. [D. E. Canning]

Most of the unusual doubleheaded diesel combinations seen are the result of a failure or other emergency conditions, as with this Class 33 and Class 50 pairing at Fairwood Junction (Westbury) on 14 September 1974. No. 50 025 had failed at Athelney with an up train from Penzance and the nearest assistance available was No. 33 004, working an inter-Regional oil train near Tiverton Junction, which assisted the train to Westbury for a fresh Type 4 to take over. [G. F. Gillham]

7E

The Class 35 'Hymeks' were delivered new by Beyer Peacock to Swindon works and after acceptance trials were put on 'shake-down' runs, usually in pairs, prior to being allocated to their depots. D7023 and D7024, with smart green paintwork still unmarked, wait to leave Swindon in 1962, soon after delivery to Western Region. As was customary on running-in turns, they are being worked in tandem, with crews on each locomotive. [Norman E. Preedy]

After a night spent shunting engineers' trains in connection with the re-laying of Tunnel Junction at Salisbury, Southern Region's D6503 and D6504 cross the newly-laid junction on their way back to Redbridge p.w. depot, October 1967. [G. F. Gillham]

One of the more unusual duties for the 'Hymeks' which should qualify for inclusion in a volume on doubleheaded diesel working in Britain, even though it involved banking, was on the celebrated Lickey incline near Bromsgrove. Class 35s worked on this duty for some time although not with conspicuous success, being used in pairs or a threesome to help northbound freight trains up the 1 in 37; D7024 and two others of the class at Blackwell, at the summit of the climb in the 1960s. Up to a dozen freights a day still called for the use of the three 'helpers'. [D. E. Canning]

Class 35 D7045, from Old Oak Common, heads back to the London Division in harness with 'Warship' D827 *Kelly* on an up express at Newbury, July 1966. With dissimilar transmissions and controls, these two diesel-hydraulic designs could not be operated other than in tandem. [G. Gore]

An unusual combination of a Class 25 and a 'Hymek' enlivened the usual variety of locomotives passing through Newbury on 31 July 1975 – No. 25 452 (ex 7502) hauling No. 7017 westward, en route to Taunton. On the side of the diesel-hydraulic beside the BR emblem can be seen the initials of the locomotive's new owners, D&EG (the Diesel & Electric Group) whose praiseworthy efforts to purchase a 'Hymek' for preservation had been successful. It is destined for work on the newly revived line to Minehead. [D. E. Canning]

Rival of the Type 3 diesel-hydraulic was the much more numerous Class 37 of 1750 hp built by English Electric. These operate in pairs quite frequently, particularly in South Wales where long and heavy loose-coupled freights are still run. They are used, too, for the iron-ore traffic from Port Talbot to the Spencer steelworks at Llanwern, in which massive trains of up to twenty 100-ton wagons are run – probably the heaviest loads yet worked in Britain. Here Nos. 37 301 and 37 304 haul one of these trains through Newport on 24 April 1975. [P. D. Hawkins]

In the old Cardiff Valleys division, the 1750 hp and 50 ton brake force of the 37s is put to good use and such oddities as brake tenders are now almost superfluous. Quite a number of the many units of the class allocated to Canton depot work in multiple, as with D6975 and D6973 photographed in Aberbeeg yard after a snow shower in January 1971. [South Devon Railway Museum]

Doubleheading is common with the numerous heavy block trains of oil tanks run on BR throughout the country. Here, a pair of Class 37s pass Greenhill Lower signal box with a formidable load from the nearby Grangemouth Oil Terminal, bound for the ICI works at Ardrossan on the Ayrshire coast; 17 September 1974. [D. G. Cameron]

Diesel fumes beat back from the road overbridge at Bromsgrove as Class 37s Nos. 37 205 and 37 307 add their tractive effort to the rear of a freight moving off up Lickey. At the head are two Class 20s; 26 April 1975. The sturdy 37s were found to be far better suited to work on Lickey than the diesel-hydraulic Type 3s now extinct.
[D. E. Canning]

Class 37 Nos. 37 216 and 37 242 passing Aspatria signal box on 8 July 1975 with train 4E36 from Workington, consisting of steel-billet empty bogies. [M. J. Jackson]

Class 37 Nos. 6868 and 6899 doubleheading an air-braked train of 26 laden coal hoppers on the curve by York station, 21 March 1972. [Norman E. Preedy]

37
21

◁ Overleaf: EE Class 40s, Nos. 40 141 and 40 170 under the wires at Guide Bridge, 21 August 1974.
[Norman E. Preedy]

Class 37s were considered for an ultra high speed service between Bristol and Paddington in the summer of 1965 and during the course of a test run the pair of Canton 37s used for these runs were re-routed via the Berks & Hants line due to a derailment near Swindon. D6881 and D6882 are here seen passing through Newbury on this occasion, on 21 June 1967. Normal gearing on the class permits a maximum of 90 mph.
[D. E. Canning]

A pair of Class 40s approaching Ais Gill summit southbound on 10 February 1973 with a heavy train of sheeted hoppers laden with anhydrite from the Long Meg quarries near Appleby. These are the heaviest freights regularly worked over the Settle & Carlisle route and run to the ICI works at Widnes. [D. E. Canning]

Excess motive power returning home to a Yorkshire depot is probably the reason for this Class 47 leading a Class 40 over the newly ballasted up line near the north end of Blea Moor Tunnel on the Settle & Carlisle line, September 1974. [D. E. Canning]

A Class 40 (No. 40 139) and a Class 25 (No. 25 049) team up with a Carlisle - Workington freight and are seen passing Aspatria station on 7 July 1975. As in other cases, this is a doubleheader not for tonnage reasons but as a result of an unbalanced working which leaves the locomotive spare but in the wrong place for its next duty. Standardisation enables locomotive diagrams to be used to the utmost advantage and accounts for the very wide range of operations of motive power today. [M. J. Jackson]

Class 40 D364 gives a helping hand to Deltic No. 9001 *St. Paddy* on 5 September 1973 after the failure of one of the latter's engines. The train is the 14.00 Kings Cross to Aberdeen and is here seen leaving Peterborough. The Class 55 remains on the train to operate the air conditioning system – a development of the future when the Class 40s were built.
[Norman E. Preedy]

The Class 42/43 'Warships' were frequently seen in the late 1960s doubleheading certain West of England expresses on Western Region, at a time when timetable accelerations were called for but which the 2700 hp 'Westerns', unaided, could not cope with except on severely shortened trains. With over 4400 hp available, two 'Warships' in multiple could easily maintain their 90 mph permitted maximum and also could make rapid recovery from any signal or p.w. checks. Here D829 *Magpie* and D827 *Kelly* slam through Newbury on the fast road with the 16.30 to Penzance. [D. E. Canning]

Rain shrouds Newbury station as the up 'Limited' sweeps through towards Paddington behind a pair of 'Warships', in 1969. Regular multiple working of these diesel-hydraulics from Laira ended with the summer service that year – the 'Cornish Riviera' being the last express they were used on – when train loads were reduced to a standard formation of nine coaches for Plymouth and beyond. [D. Bullock]

Class 42 'Warship' D819 *Goliath* doubleheads Class 45 D85 (now 45 109) on a train for Leeds, seen waiting for the 'right away' at Dawlish station on 28 July 1971. [Norman E. Preedy]

D819
1F37

D821 *Greyhound* and D827 *Kelly* on 17 June 1968 in the bay at Newbury West after being taken off the down 'Cornish Riviera' with brake trouble. This was during the period the Western Region was double-heading selected West of England expresses with paired 'Warships'. [D. E. Canning]

A rare doubleheader at Reading, with D859 *Vanquisher* piloting the solitary Brush-built D0280 *Falcon* on the 9 a.m. Paddington to Bristol. Built in 1961 and remaining the property of the manufacturers until taken into BR stock in 1970, this locomotive was allocated to Bath Road from 1965 onwards and was a regular on Bristol - Paddington trains from then until the introduction of air-braked stock in 1969. Of 2800 hp, with two Maybach engines, it had the highest maximum designed speed (100 mph) of any diesel on Western Region. [D. E. Canning]

D806 *Centaur* and D822 *Hercules* easing through Thatcham on 12 December 1970 with the 'Cornish Riviera' to run wrong line to Newbury. Below, D819 *Goliath* and D827 *Kelly* crossing over for single-line working from Ufton Crossing to Thatcham with a Penzance express on another Sunday in December of that year.

[D. E. Canning

No. 832 *Onslaught* and No. 805 *Benbow* run leisurely through Dawlish Warren on their way from Exeter to Laira depot during a lull in the flow of holiday trains to the west, 21 August 1972. Both had been on SR duties and were coming to Laira to help with the WR peak holiday traffic. [David H. Allan]

A powerful combination of Class 46 No. 46 002 and Class 47 No. 47 001 accelerate through the former site of Marazion station in West Cornwall with the 14.00 to Birmingham, after a late start from Penzance; 17 July 1974. [G. F. Gillham]

'Warship' and 'Peak'; Class 42 D817 *Foxhound* and Class 45 No. 98 *Royal Engineer* on the climb away from Torquay with the up 'Cornishman' bound for Bradford, 17 June 1971. The Class 45 will work right through but the 'Warship' will come off at Bristol.
[G. F. Gillham]

1013

0000

Reading, 19 April 1973; Class 47 No. 1741 from Cardiff (Canton) pilots Class 52 No. 1071 *Western Renown* on the 10.07 Cardiff - Paddington. Both locomotives look as grimy and uncared for as industrial shunters. [G. F. Gillham]

Having failed at Thatcham whilst working a Newbury - Reading local freight, Class 31 No. 31 117 is helped by No. 47 090 summoned from Reading to assist; 11 September 1975.

Below; No. 47 082, minus its nameplate, and No. 47 137 crossing from the up to the down line at Savernake on 16 May 1976 *en route* to Westbury after working engineers' trains. [D. E. Canning]

Control has added a spare northbound Class 25 to the normal head-end power of a Class 47 on the 'Royal Scot' on 28 July 1967, photographed in the Lune valley to the south of Tebay. There is no headboard – such as BR once favoured in the days before such individual frills were thought out of keeping with the modern image – merely the code 1S57 to show this is the premier express of the day. Both units are in the two-tone green which was both serviceable and smart-looking. [D. M. Cox]

A pair of Brush Class 47s in multiple make a formidable 5500 hp combination and well able to handle any normally permitted service load. Nos. 1688 and 1743, from Canton and Tyseley respectively, pause at Bristol (Temple Meads) on a Saturday in July 1970 with a Paignton - Manchester train.

[D. E. Canning]

The up end of Exeter (St. Davids), 29 June 1974; another Paignton - Manchester train is headed by Class 31/1 No. 31 299 and Class 47/4 No. 47 481. The smaller of these Brush-built locomotives was formerly at Immingham (No. 5655 prior to renumbering) but had been transferred to Bath Road depot some time before the date of this photograph. [Norman E. Preedy]

Class 47 Nos. 1854 and 1910, working in multiple on a heavy coal train, traverse the down line of the Dartford loop, between Mottingham and New Eltham; 11 August 1973.
[Brian Morrison]

Perhaps the best known example of consistent doubleheading on BR was the use of the Class 50s in pairs on Anglo-Scottish expresses on the northern extension of the electrified section of the West Coast main line. Initially they worked north of Crewe, or north of Preston after this became the changeover point when the section up to there was switched in. D407 and D411 here surmount the worst of Shap with ease on the northbound 'Royal Scot' in August 1970. [D. E. Canning]

◁
First and second generation English Electric Type 4s; Class 50 No. 50 036 pilots Class 40 No. 211 *Mauretania* with the 10.15 Euston - Bangor out of Crewe. This service is used as a running-in turn for ex-works diesels, in this case No. 50 036. [P. D. Hawkins]

Class 50 Nos. 50 021 and No. 434 (still not yet renumbered 50 034) leaving Glasgow Central with the 13.55 to Euston, February 1974. Inauguration of the full electric service is not far away at this date and the pairs of 50s will disappear as standard express motive power over Shap. [D. G. Cameron]

Another view of the same pair of Class 50s, departing for Crewe, in February 1974. Amongst other design refinements, these locomotives are equipped for rapid coupling/uncoupling in connection with use singly or in multiple. However, they cannot be used, except in tandem, with any other class, as their square orange-coloured coupling symbol shows. [D. G. Cameron]

The value of the 5400 hp available from two class 50s was not so much speed or the weight of trains as the ability to recover time after the numerous slacks and restrictions along the West Coast route due to electrification work. Some really spirited running, well up to the 100 mph of the design, has been recorded in making up lost time caused by checks. This scene shows Nos. 50 039 and 50 025 (leading) at speed near Shap on 2 April 1974 with the up 'Royal Scot'. [Brian Morrison]

Another Anglo-Scottish express, this time northbound, with No. 50 036 leading No. 60 038 shortly before the full service of 'Electric Scots' commenced to Glasgow in mid-1974. In contrast to the bridge opposite, this one has not had to be raised to give clearance for the catenary, one of the very many expensive features involved in overhead electrification of an existing line. [Brian Morrison]

1M19

Class 50s in pairs became quite a familiar sight and sound on the scenic Settle & Carlisle line during the period that Anglo-Scottish expresses were diverted as a result of engineers' occupation of the main line as electrification proceeded. Nos. 423 and 410 'hoover' their way up to Ais Gill summit with an express for Euston in July 1973. Above, Nos. 414 and 435 on the same date with another southbound express, leaving Birkett Tunnel on the climb to Ais Gill. [R. H. Leslie]

No question of multiple control in this instance of doubleheading, with very contrasting Type 4s putting out a mixed Sulzer-Maybach roar as the drivers work up to full throttle . . . The scene is Bodmin Road in Cornwall, with a severe upgrade facing trains leaving the station here, plus sharp curves. Heading is No. 47 122 and 'in the shafts' – to use a steam term from another day and age – is D1034 *Western Dragoon,* with the up 'Cornish Riviera' on a Sunday in September 1975. In terms of sheer ability to move off an adverse load, the diesel-hydraulic has the edge, having greater torque; indeed a savagely driven 'Western' could burn rails so badly from a standing start that one of the devices fitted to them in later years slowed down the speed with which the driver could turn on the power.
[P. D. Hawkins]

D 1041 *Western Prince* piloting D 1058 *Western Nobleman* with the six-coach 14.00 Penzance-Birmingham at St. Erth, 30 July 1975. Externally, D 1058 looks ready for retirement but can still do her share . . .This daily doubleheader is due to an unbalanced working, returning one locomotive spare to Laira depot.
[Brian Morrison]

D1051 *Western Ambassador* and D1023 *Western Fusilier* show their mastery of Lickey bank with the 'Western Enterprise' enthusiasts' rail tour run on 27 April 1975. [G. F. Bannister]

Penzance, 29 August 1973; D1048 *Western Lady* backs into the carriage sidings whilst D1059 *Western Empire* and D1008 *Western Harrier* draw away from the platform in a haze of exhaust fumes, bound for Paddington. [P. D. Hawkins]